The Ultimate LinkedIn Guide

by Neo Monefa

Table of Contents

1. What is LinkedIn?

The History of LinkedIn

LinkedIn began as a small project in Reid Hoffman's living room in 2002. With him were Allen Blue, Jean-Luc Valliant, Eric Ly and Konstantin Guericke. After spending the rest of the year developing, testing and fine-tuning the professional networking site, the team officially launched LinkedIn on May 5, 2003, a day they affectionately refer to as Cinco de LinkedIn.

Upon launching, Reid Hoffman's team initially invited 300 of their friends and by the end of its first month, there were already over 4,500 registered profiles on LinkedIn. Sequoia Capital, a venture capitalist, invested over $4 million dollars on LinkedIn on October of 2003. By the end of the year, the site already had over 80,000 and 18 employees.

The rapid rise in the number of LinkedIn members can be attributed to the site's unique layout and platform. Members were able to showcase their skills, experience and qualifications without having to divulge any irrelevant personal information as was the trend of other social networking sites in that period. By April of 2004, LinkedIn announced that it has reached the half a million members' milestone, an impressive achievement for a website that was less than a year old.

In October of the same year, the company received an additional $10 million in investment funding from Greylock. By year's end, LinkedIn had over 1.6 million members – half of which were from outside the United States, and the company had 33 employees.

In 2005, LinkedIn launched two key services that added a wide variety of features for its members. The first was LinkedIn Jobs which was launched in March 2005. This allowed companies to post job opportunities for the site's members. The second was the subscription services for both individual members and businesses.

Throughout 2006, LinkedIn expanded its network of jobseekers, suppliers and businesses. By the end of 2007, the site already had over 15 million users. There are now over 147 million LinkedIn users from over 300 countries worldwide. The site continues to provide its members essential features that allow its users to form meaningful professional connections using a social networking platform.

In the next section, we will look closer at the objectives of LinkedIn and what it aims to achieve for its members. It is very much different from other social networking sites such as Facebook and Google+ in the sense that personal information takes a backseat to professional qualifications. Was this LinkedIn's primary purpose? Let's find out.

LinkedIn's Objectives

There are no limitations as to who can join LinkedIn. However, only a small number of its users are able to use the site to its highest potential. But what exactly is LinkedIn meant to be? In this section, we will be looking at the purpose and objective of LinkedIn and how you can use this platform to your professional advantage.

1.   To help you establish a professional profile online

LinkedIn is similar to a curriculum vitae in the sense that you will be able to showcase your professional experiences, skills and background. The main differences are that with LinkedIn, your page can be searched for on Google and your profile can be visible to millions of other users.

A lot of businesses are turning to the Internet when searching for suppliers or employees to fulfill their corporate or professional needs. Having a LinkedIn profile will give you a definite advantage to potential employers because they can simply search for you online and they will be able to see a comprehensive page on the site with all the information that they need to know about you.

2.   To keep you in touch with your colleagues and friends in the business

The nature of business and employment is always in flux. Most professionals jump from one company to another while some meet hundreds of people per year due to the nature of their jobs. LinkedIn makes it possible and easy for you to connect with old co-workers, new contacts and suppliers within the site. You will be able to see their updated contact information, new projects, professional updates and more.

3.   To give you a place where you can exchange ideas or find expert opinions

LinkedIn is no longer just a professional networking site, it has become a community where all the members from all over the world can participate and share ideas or let their opinions be known. If you are in need of expert advice, you will be able to easily find one (or a hundred) whom you can send a message to or contact directly. If you run out of ideas for your latest business project, you can use LinkedIn's features to connect with your network or a wider community for an impromptu brainstorming.

4.   To expand your employment and/or business opportunities

LinkedIn makes it easy for its members to find their professional needs, whether it's a better employment opportunities, new clients or potential investors. You will also be able to build a powerful professional reputation through your network and contacts. LinkedIn also has a reliable and efficient search engine tool that will help you find what you need faster and more effectively.

A lot of people take LinkedIn for granted. Not all of its members are able to utilize and take advantage of the site's features to its maximum potential. One reason for this is that they don't know just how much LinkedIn can benefit their careers and businesses.

We will explore the different advantages of using LinkedIn as your professional profile and as a way to search for employment opportunities that you are qualified for.

Advantages of Using LinkedIn

While other more prominent social networking sites such as Facebook and Twitter often take center stage when discussing online networking, LinkedIn has been quietly and efficiently working in the background.

On LinkedIn, the main focus is your professional life. Your last vacation, honeymoon or reunion with high school classmates takes a backseat on this site. The most effective way to use LinkedIn to your advantage is to showcase what prospective employers want to see and what you want the world to know about you as a professional.

Just how can LinkedIn help you meet your personal, professional and business goals? Here are some of the advantages of using this networking site.

LinkedIn allows you to build your credibility through your network. It is often difficult for job applicants to show their credibility in just one or two pages of a resume. Without a proper interview or one-on-one, the recruiter will have to rely on the short summary of your career and skills. Often, this process does not effectively convey what the applicant can do for the company.

If you are a professional looking for better career opportunities, LinkedIn helps you establish your credibility through your profile and your network. Your network will be able to introduce and connect you with their network and contacts. Remember the saying "it's not *what* you know but *who* you know"? In LinkedIn, you will be able to have easier access to your contacts' network of colleagues, partners and friends in the industry.

These are the types of connections that you can take advantage of in LinkedIn that other social networking sites do not offer.

How your network will be put to use is entirely up to you. If you will be using LinkedIn for your business, this robust network can help you in lead generation or in searching for ideal suppliers. If you are a professional looking for employment opportunities, your network may have the opening that you are looking for.

LinkedIn Connections focus on quality and not on quantity. In most social networking sites, you are able to freely add friends and contacts even if you have not met each other personally before. In LinkedIn, before you are able to add a contact, you will need to indicate and specify how you know the other person.

You can use the Personal Note feature to refresh their memory.

If you want to add someone to your contacts even if you haven't personally met before, it's important to reference how you learned about that person (e.g. through LinkedIn news, a common friend, a colleague, etc.). This will help you build and protect your credibility and to avoid being tagged as a spammer.

Get up-to-date industry news and tips. Professionals who are always looking to improve their skills and to make better decisions spend hours scouring the Internet for relevant news and professional tips. On LinkedIn, these are delivered to your own LinkedIn backend page every day. You will be able to customize the news topics that you will receive from top reliable sources.

You will be able to save time and effort searching for relevant news updates from a wide variety of sources. You can also share these articles to your network or save them for future reference.

LinkedIn lets you easily track company updates. For professionals looking for employment opportunities in specific companies, this feature will make it easier to know what the company is up to, who has been recently hired or let go and its available job postings. You can follow multiple companies at a time and their updates are presented in a linear and clear manner.

You will also be able to share the updates or leave comments – a great way to show your interest in the company.

üü **You can use your contacts for just about anything.** The great thing about having contacts that have their own skills and professional niches is that you can ask for help or advice for just about any project, topic or decision. You can start your own group and invite the contacts that you think can help you with what you need. The simpler method is to update your status and encourage your contacts to participate in a discussion.

There are hundreds of ways for you to use LinkedIn to your advantage. In later chapters, you will learn about how you can make your profile stand out from the rest. You will also learn how to utilize LinkedIn's features to help you showcase your skills, career and work experience. For now however, let us look at the people who are using LinkedIn.

In the next section, we will briefly look at the demographics of LinkedIn members. This will help you understand the type of professionals that frequently uses the site for networking purposes. You will also be able to get an idea of your employment opportunities as we look at the number and types of businesses that use LinkedIn to post available job openings in their company.

The LinkedIn Demographics

There are now over 150 million LinkedIn members from all over the world according to the latest statistics released by the company. LinkedIn is now the second most visited and used social networking site behind Facebook. Let us look at a rough breakdown of this massive number.

Over 60 million of the registered users are located in the United States, followed by India with 14 million members. North America is still the region with the most active members with 63.7 million followed by Europe with 32.9 million.

Over 40% of all members are between 35 to 54 years old and 53% of all users are male.

The job function that is most prevalent among members is entrepreneurship with 10.8% of all users, followed by sales with 9.5%. The industry that is most represented is technology with 14.3% of all member, followed by finance and manufacturing with 12.4% and 10.1% respectively.

Up to 39% of the total number of members (roughly 58.5 million) lists themselves as part of upper management. They are managers, owners, directors, chief officers or vice presidents.

All Fortune 500 companies have at least one representative on LinkedIn acting on behalf of the organization.

2. How to Use LinkedIn

Social networking has become an essential tool in connecting old friends, distant relatives, classmates in middle school and co-workers from years past. One great use of social networking is to connect job applicants with prospective employers who are looking for professionals to join their team.

LinkedIn is one of the most widely used social networking platforms that focus on professional connections. If you are a professional looking for better employment opportunities or simply looking to connect with other professionals in your field, LinkedIn is a platform that could benefit your career and employment. LinkedIn is also a great avenue for businesses to find the professionals that they need to complete their ranks or to promote their company to potential buyers and suppliers.

In this chapter, we will explore the basics of the LinkedIn network, starting with a brief review of its history. We will also touch on the fundamental objectives of LinkedIn and how you can take advantage of this for your own purpose. If you are a skilled professional looking to get noticed by companies, the following sections will show you how LinkedIn has risen in the ranks of the most popular social networking sites. You will also learn more about what the site has to offer and why it's important to have a LinkedIn account if you want your professional life to flourish.

Now that you know a bit of LinkedIn's background. It's now time to dive into the professional networking platform and to present your professional acuities to the corporate world. In this chapter, we will be exploring the basics of how to get started on LinkedIn, beginning with your own profile.

Creating a Profile in LinkedIn

If you already have an account in social networking sites such as Facebook, Twitter or Google+, then you won't have any difficulties in creating a LinkedIn profile.

The first and most obvious step to get started is to go to LinkedIn's homepage at http://www.linkedin.com/.

The homepage is pretty straightforward. This is the page that you will see when you want to log in to your account. You can also search for existing LinkedIn members through this page.

Let's create your account. Start by filling out the form and then click on the green 'Join Now' button when you're done.

It is always best to use your real name on LinkedIn. If most of your professional contacts know you through your nickname or other moniker, you can use that as well. Just remember that this is the name that your prospective employers will see when you submit your application for a job posting.

After clicking the 'Join Now' button, you will be taken to the next page where you will be asked to fill out another form. This time, you will give general details about your location and your job description.

Don't forget to fill out the required fields before moving on to the next page!

You have three options to choose from for your profile: Employed, Job Seeker or Student. If you are currently employed, you will be asked to mention your job title and the company that you are working for. If you are self-employed, simply tick on the small box and you will be asked to choose the industry that you are a part of.

Scroll down to see the rest of the list.

Choose the industry that best describes what you do or the services that you offer and cater to. If you serve more than one industry, choose the one where most of your work comes from. You can always tweak your profile later on to add the other industries that you are a part of.

If you intend to use LinkedIn as a tool to look for job opportunities, select the Job Seeker option. You will then be asked to give a very brief history of your last employment. If you are or were self-employed, you will again be asked to choose your industry.

If you chose the Student option, you will be asked your college or institution and the dates that you attended.

Once you have completed all the required fields, simply click on the 'Create my profile' button to move on to the next step.

The next page gives you the option to store an e-mail address with LinkedIn. This will be where updates to your profiles, private messages, reports and other correspondences from LinkedIn will be sent. You can skip this step if you wish to add your e-mail address at a later time. Simply click on the 'Skip this step' link to proceed to the next page.

The next step is to confirm the e-mail address that you registered with. This is essential if you want to create a profile on LinkedIn. An e-mail confirmation will prove that you are not a bot or automated spammer.

After confirming your e-mail, the next page will show you some of your contacts from your e-mail account that is already on LinkedIn. You can begin adding people on your contacts list from this page. LinkedIn will also show you contact suggestions that you can include in your list.

The next page will tell if you were able to successfully establish your profile. You have the option to share your LinkedIn profile to your Facebook contacts and Twitter followers. You will also be given a URL or link to your page, which you can add to your blog, e-mail signature and other online tools.

Now that your account has been registered with LinkedIn, you now have to choose your plan level. LinkedIn gives you the option to make a free profile with limited features. Premium accounts have more features, which can help you with your professional purposes more.

If you choose the Basic account, you always have the option to upgrade later on.

Congratulations! You now have a LinkedIn account. Now the real work needs to be taken care of. When you arrive on your LinkedIn homepage, you will initially see a very blank profile with limited information.

Take note of your to-do list on the right side. Use this as your guide in creating a comprehensive LinkedIn profile.

Only the information that you provided on the account set up is visible. Don't worry, you can easily edit this page to showcase your professional credentials.

First, mouse over the Profile link on the menu bar on the top part of the page. On the drop-down menu, choose Edit Profile.

You will be brought to the page where you can edit the details on your profile. This is essentially the area where you will be adding the details that you want your contacts to know about you. In later chapters, you will be given tips and tricks on how to make your profile more interesting for employers.

Don't get overwhelmed with the amount of information that you will need to put in. Remember that you don't have to mention every little professional detail, though it is advisable that you include all relevant information that employers will be interested in.

Let's briefly touch on your profile information by section.

The first section provides a short introduction for the rest of your profile. This is the first thing that other people will see when they view your profile.

The fields that you see above are not required but it will be to your advantage to make your profile as "meaty" as possible. When uploading a photo, be sure to use an image where you appear as professional as possible.

The Recommendations field is one of the best ways to catch an employer's attention. When you click on the "+Ask for a recommendation" link, you will be taken to this page:

You can request a recommendation from your previous or present colleagues or bosses, friends, former clients and so on.

Adding connections is simply searching for other LinkedIn members who are on your address book. You can use all your e-mail accounts to search for professional connections who you can invite to join your network. We will discuss this at length in the next section.

You can also customize the URL of your profile page. This is extremely helpful in getting visitors to your page by simply searching for your name on Google or any other search engine. To maximize exposure, use your first and last name and avoid using special characters and intentional misspellings.

Double-check your spelling before setting your custom URL.

Prepare alternatives in case that your preferred URL is already taken.

The next parts are called "sections". These are the areas where you can highlight a skill or your previous job experience. You can add the sections that you feel are most relevant to what you want to present to the corporate world. Simply click on the Add Sections link.

You will then see a popup box containing all the sections that you can add to your page. You can also add applications like SlideShare

Presentation, E-Bookshelf and WordPress. In a later chapter, we will look at the most essential applications that can help bring your profile page to the next level.

The next parts that you want to pay attention to is the Summary, Work Experience and Education portions. Much like in a resume or curriculum vitae, these are critical details that every employer looks at.

The Summary is simply a short description of your professional experience and career goals. No need to write a novella here, anything that is concise (preferably less than 500 words) and direct-to-the-point will be appreciated by your page visitors.

Be honest in the Experiences that you include in your page. If you have very little experience in your industry, don't invent positions and companies. Just include what employers can easily verify.

The last part that we will be looking at deals with more personal information and your skills. Be sure to avoid revealing too much information. Remember that you want your page to be as professional as possible.

Your contact preferences basically let your page visitors know what they can contact you for. If you want to limit your LinkedIn correspondences to just career opportunities and business deals, you can exclude all other reasons by editing your preferences.

Another important area that you should pay attention to is the Skills & Expertise box.

Some employers may simply search for potential applicants based on their skills or area of expertise, so it's essential for you to include any of your relevant skill. You can add as many as you want, but don't go overboard. Only include the skills that you are capable of and expertise that you have experience with.

Now that your profile is filled with your professional details, photo and experiences, it's now time to invite your contacts and business associates to your network. We will explore how you can do this in the next section.

Adding and Importing Contacts in LinkedIn

In order for your LinkedIn profile to reach its highest potential, you need to be strategic in the people that you invite as your contacts. Remember that in LinkedIn, connections are all about quality and not quantity. In this section, you will learn how to add and import contacts from your e-mails' address book, as well as how to search for contacts in LinkedIn.

The first method that we will discuss is using your e-mails' address books.

There are two ways for you to get started. One option is to go to the 'Contacts' link on the menu bar and then click on Add Connections from the drop-down menu.

The second option is to simply click on the 'Add Connections' link from the upper right corner of the screen.

Either method will bring you to the Import Contacts page.

Again, you have two options to add contacts through e-mail. The first is to enter your email address on the field. This will give LinkedIn permission to access the address book of the e-mail that you provided.
After clicking the 'Continue' button, a new window will open and you will be asked to log in to your e-mail account. Upon logging in, LinkedIn will ask for your permission to access your address book. Confirm this request to import your contacts.

Once LinkedIn has access to your address book, it will give you a list of your address book contacts that are already on LinkedIn.

Choose the contacts that you wish to add to your personal LinkedIn network by ticking on the box beside their profile photos. When you're done choosing, click the 'Add Connection(s)' button to move on to the next step. On the next page, you will see a list of people in your address book that are not yet on LinkedIn. You have the option to invite them to create their own accounts.

The second option that you can use to invite contacts is to manually type out e-mail addresses on the right side of the Add Contacts page.

This option will automatically send LinkedIn invitations to the e-mail addresses that you list down.
If you want to add your colleagues from work that is already on LinkedIn, the steps are very simple.

Go back to the Import Contacts page and choose the 'Colleagues' tab.

If your company has its own LinkedIn account and page, you will be able to see other employees who listed your company as their employer. If you own the company that you work and you don't have a LinkedIn page for your business yet, you will not be able to see contact suggestions.

Alternatively, you can also search for old classmates or people you went to school with by clicking on the 'Alumni' tab.

On the 'People You May Know' tab, you will be shown thumbnails of some of your address book contacts that you haven't added yet and their networks and contacts that are in the same industry as you are or may gone to the same school as you did.

A more straightforward way to search for contacts is through the LinkedIn search bar.

Just type in the name of the person that you want to look for and press the blue button beside the field. You can also use this feature to look for companies and job postings.
On LinkedIn, having meaningful professional connections will increase your success in whatever you want to use the site for. Whether it's for finding better job opportunities or searching for

clients and partners, your contacts will broaden your reach through their networks.

How to Search and Apply For Job Openings on LinkedIn

More and more professionals are turning to social networking platforms to search for employment opportunities. In 2014 alone, over 10 million signed up to LinkedIn as a jobseeker. You may think that competition is tough on the site but opportunities abound as over 70 companies in the Fortune 500 and plenty other smaller and more localized ones regularly use the LinkedIn for hiring solutions.

To begin your job search, highlight the 'Jobs' link on the menu bar and then click on 'Find Jobs'.

You will be taken to the Jobs Home page where you will be able to search for jobs using keywords, job titles, company names or industry.

After typing in your search term, click on the blue 'Search' button to arrive at the search results page. If you want to limit the search results to a specific location, industry or job posting date, click on the 'Advanced' link under the 'Search' button to set your search parameters.

You will be taken to the Advanced Search page where you will see different search settings that you can adjust, depending on your preferences.

This will help you filter out the jobs that you're not interested in or are qualified for, saving you time and effort. You can either search for jobs using keywords, job title or preferred location using the search functions on the first part of the page.
Alternatively, you can catch a wider net by searching for specific job functions, required experience and industry.

You can tick as many relevant boxes as you want for the job function, experience and industry. If you paid for a Premium

LinkedIn account, you will also be able to indicate your preferred salary range. To see all the available job listings, tick the boxes for All Job Functions, Any Level and All Industries.

Once you've set your search parameters or have entered your keywords, you will be taken to the search results page where all the relevant job postings will be listed.

Take note of the fields highlighted by the red box. If you are overwhelmed with the results of your search, you can narrow down the list using several refine search tools provided.

If you see a job posting that you're interested in, simply click on the linked job title and you will be taken to the page where you will be shown more details about the listing.

If you feel that you are qualified for the job and you're interested in applying, you can either click on the 'Apply Now' button at the bottom of the page or the button on the upper right side.

After clicking the 'Apply Now' button, a popup box will appear. Here, you will be able to set the main e-mail address where the company can reach you, upload a cover letter and/or resume and double-check other details that will be seen by the recruiter.

Before clicking on the 'Submit' button, ensure that all the required fields are filled out. After submitting, you will receive a confirmation that the job poster has received your application.

To review your submitted applications, go back to the Jobs Home page and click on the 'Saved Jobs' tab.

On the Saved Jobs page, you will be able to review the job openings that you applied for, as well as other job listings that you have saved while searching.

If you come across job listings that you're interested in but don't feel like applying for just yet, you have the option to save that job post for a later review.

To save job listings from the search results page, simply highlight the posting that you're interested in. Click on the 'Save job' link which will appear on the right side of the listing.

To view your saved jobs, simply follow the steps outlined earlier for viewing the jobs that you applied for.

There are no limits to the number of job postings that you can apply for. In the next section, we will explore some LinkedIn tips and tricks that would help make your applications more successful. We will also look at the different ways you can maximize your profile space to get it noticed by employers and other LinkedIn members.

3. Maximizing and Promoting Your LinkedIn Profile

Now that your LinkedIn profile boasts of your skills, experience and other important professional details, it's time to get your page noticed by your network.

You won't always use your LinkedIn account as a job hunting tool. Once you get the job you want, your LinkedIn profile will remain active. Don't abandon it and allow it to be buried under millions of other profiles. You can still use your page to further your career and to be better at your job.

Simply having a profile and filling out minimal fields about yourself will not help you get mileage out of your network. In the next section, we'll look at the different reasons why building and maintaining an extensive and informative LinkedIn profile is important for your professional career.

Importance of Having a Complete LinkedIn Profile

Your main purpose of registering in LinkedIn may be simply for discovering career and employment opportunities. But did you know that you can use LinkedIn for much, much more?

After finding your dream job on LinkedIn, it's in your best interest to continue updating your page with relevant professional information – either about what you do or what your company is up to. Other reasons why you should maintain the completeness and attractiveness of your LinkedIn profile include:

You will be 40 times more likely to receive professional opportunities. More companies are turning to LinkedIn's networks for headhunting and recruitment services. Having a complete and accurate profile will attract more employers to your page because the details that they need to know about you are already in plain view.

They will be quicker to decide whether you have the right skills and qualification for what they need.

You will get more accurate job offers. Despite the tough competition in the available workforce on LinkedIn, employers are still eager to invite qualified members for interviews or further correspondences. While this is good for applicants, quality still trumps quantity, even in job hunting. If your profile is incomplete, you may get contacted for jobs that you may over or under qualified for. On some occasions, you may even receive offers for jobs that have no relevance to your skills or experience at all. To prevent this from happening (and wasting your time), invest in establishing accurate and complete details on your profile.

It will be easier to establish your credibility. In business and employment, first impressions can dictate whether a person is worth their time and investment. Your LinkedIn profile is a reflection of who you are and how you conduct yourself and your business. If you have an incomplete profile, your page's viewers may think that you are not professional or reliable. You want to put your best foot forward right at the onset and on LinkedIn, this begins with your profile.

It will be easier to find you. When employers, business suppliers and networks look for people with specific skills or qualifications, all they'll need to do is to make a quick search using LinkedIn's search function. Those who have complete profiles are more likely to end up at the top of the search results and they have more chances of being offered a career or business opportunity. Google also includes LinkedIn profiles in their search results. If you want to make it easier for other people to find, all it takes is a complete profile.

Completing your profile is not difficult. In fact, you can finish all the required fields in less than an hour. LinkedIn also provides you with a checklist and guide to determine whether your profile has all the necessary and relevant fields filled out.

You will be able to see this on your Edit Profile page.

In the next section, we will discuss how to make your profile grab the attention of the people who will be able to offer you great professional and career opportunities. We will also look at how you will be able to maximize LinkedIn's features to your advantage.

How to Attract the Attention of Potential Employers

When you submit an application for job listings on LinkedIn, the employers will check out your profile to see whether you match the requirements that they are looking for. How will you be able to show to show that you're the best person for the job? By using LinkedIn's features to showcase the relevance of your skills and experiences, the employers will be able to gauge your strengths, attributes and qualifications.

In this section, we will explore the different methods that you can employ in order to make your profile more attractive for potential employers. Whether you are actively applying for job openings or just waiting to be found, your profile will be the ultimate source of interest for the services that you are offering.

Follow these simple and essential tips to make your LinkedIn profile standout.

Tip #1: Write a winning headline.

All LinkedIn profiles come equipped with headlines that you can edit and change. Headlines are great for making a short introduction of yourself and what you can bring to the table. To change your headline, follow these steps:

First, go to your Edit Profile page and then click on the 'Edit' link next to your name.

Once you're in your Basic Information page, click on the Headline field to change, edit or write the text that you want to appear on your headline.

Now that you know how to set up your headline, keep these guidelines in mind when writing your unique professional LinkedIn headline:

Be concise. Long headlines are tedious to read and do nothing to attract attention. When writing your headline, go directly to the point of what you want to convey.

Make it marketable. Remember that you are essentially trying to market yourself to employers and your headline should make them want to check you out.

Add value. To add value, try to be as specific as possible. For example, *"Helping businesses reach their sales targets"* is not nearly as good as *"Helping start up businesses achieve their online sales goals through social networking campaigns"*.

Highlight unique skills and experiences. You will have thousands of competition on LinkedIn so you'll need to highlight what you have that the others don't.

Research and use keywords. Google has a free keyword tool that you can use for research. Look for different combinations that you can use for your headline. Keywords will make your search ranking higher, which basically means, more exposure for your profile.

Do not rely on clichés and buzzwords. Millions of LinkedIn headlines are littered with industry jargon and buzzwords that don't mean anything. Set yourself apart by using simple and smart words instead of clichés.

When you're done creating your headline, simply click on the 'Save Changes' button and go to your profile page to see how your headline looks.

You are still the best judge of whether your profile looks good or not. If something doesn't read or feel right, change it. Go with your gut and instincts. Having confidence on your LinkedIn profile is beneficial for you and your chances of getting noticed.

Tip #2: Use the Summary portion to highlight your skills and capabilities.

The Summary on your LinkedIn profile is typically used to convey the user's aspirations and goals. While this is a good way to deliver a message to potential employers, this space is better utilized for highlighting your skills, services and your work processes.

Include how you get your work done and how you overcome problems that may arise in your line of work. These will covey to employers that you are a reliable and resourceful worker. Again, be as concise as possible. Make your summary easy to read and understand. Most recruiters want to know as much as they can in less than a minute. If you are able to get your message across in the quickest time possible, you stand a better chance of being selected for the next step in their recruitment.

Tip #3: Be active.

Just like on Facebook or Twitter, your contacts will more likely visit your site if you regularly post updates. The same logic applies to LinkedIn. The main difference between LinkedIn and the rest is that your status updates MUST be professional in nature or something related to you, your job or your industry.

Avoid mentioning anything personal like your last date or what you had for dinner. Save those updates for Facebook. On LinkedIn, these status update guidelines will help make your profile active:

Share articles and resources. Use a URL shortening tool like Tinyurl to make the links more concise. Direct your network to breaking industry news, interesting blog articles, videos or images or websites that you think are useful. Don't think too much about whether your network will appreciate it or not, just post content that you think is valuable.

Ask questions. Make your profile come alive by starting a discussion among your contacts and network. Ask questions related to a problem that your contacts can help you with.

Mention any events, courses or programs that you have attended/will attend to generate interest. Some of your contacts may have attended the same event or are interested in expanding their knowledge. Your status update can begin a discussion of what you have learned and what others can help you with. It will also show that you are constantly honing your craft, which is a big plus for recruiters.

On the other end of the spectrum, there are guidelines on the proper LinkedIn status updates decorum. Be sure to avoid doing any of the following:

Don't blatantly advertise products, people, websites or services through your status updates. LinkedIn was not intended to be an advertising site, so don't turn it into one.

Don't update your status TOO frequently. You may feel the urge to share an article that you've read and that's fine. If you feel the urge again after an hour, restrain yourself. You want to keep your updates to just a few per day. You don't want your contacts or page visitors to think that you have nothing better to do.

Think twice about what you're posting, you might offend people. There are plenty of LinkedIn users who post offensive and subliminal materials without hesitation. Don't be like them. Tact and caution should always be used before posting anything. Just like in an office environment or a seminar with colleagues, you need to be careful of the words that you'll utter. You don't want to be seen as a callous and insensitive person, especially by potential employers.

Just like your Headline, your status updates can be a powerful tool in establishing your credibility. For best results, plan ahead. Have an idea of how many updates you want to post on a given day. Strategize and gather interesting materials. The healthier your profile is in terms of intellectual activity, the more impressed your page viewers will be.

Tip #4: Ask for recommendations.

One of the best features that LinkedIn offers is the Recommendations. In this section of your LinkedIn profile, your clients, bosses, colleagues or business partners can vouch for your skills, capabilities and ability to get the job done. Recommendations are essentially like job references.

Not having recommendations will not hurt your chances of getting noticed. Having *good* recommendations however, can help pique the interest of recruiters, especially if one or some of your recommendations were written by a common contact.

The best types of recommendations are those created by *actual* clients, bosses or colleagues that give a narrative of a specific project or projects that they did with you. How will you get these types of recommendations? By writing recommendations for others. Give meaningful recommendation in order to get some in return.

Tip #5: Know the people who want to know you.

Another great feature on LinkedIn is that it gives you basic statistics of the visitors of your page. For the free, basic account, you will be able to see the last five people who viewed your account, the number page visits in the last 90 days and the number of times that your profile appeared in search results in the last 90 days.
Visit the pages of the people you want to impress or get to know better. It may be a recruiter, a potential boss or business client or just someone in the industry that you admire. When they check out their own profile views, they will see your name and headline. We'll show you how to change your privacy settings in the next item.

Tip #6: Tweak your privacy settings for maximum exposure.

It's common wisdom to just let the world see your full profile, whether they have a LinkedIn account or not. The downside to this is that you won't be able to know for sure who's viewing your profile. The more you know about your audience, the better you'll be able to effectively construct the content of your page.

To make sure that your profile and security settings are set to benefit YOU, follow these simple steps and guidelines:

To access your settings, scroll over your name on the upper right corner any page on LinkedIn. Choose Settings from the drop down menu.

On your Account homepage, you will see your privacy and account options. Let's first adjust two things: what will be seen by the owners of the pages you'll visit and who will be able to see your page activities. We will access both from the Profile tab.

For your activity feed, choose Network. It's good to have your network see the updates on your page. Whether it's a promotion, new job or recommendations, you want them to know that you're an active professional.

Next thing that you should set is your settings for the pages that you visited. As mentioned earlier, you want to promote your page in everything that you do on LinkedIn. To do this, use the recommended setting of showing your full name and headline for other users' page views.

Another important setting that you need to pay attention to is your advertising preferences. This will limit the ways that LinkedIn can use your name and profile photo for third-party advertising. To do this, click on the 'Account' tab and then the Manage Advertising Preferences link.

All you need to do is to uncheck the box that gives LinkedIn your permission to use your content for third-party advertising.

Feel free to explore other settings that you want to edit to suit your privacy preferences. To see whether you like the settings that you're using, log off your LinkedIn account and visit your page. You will see your profile the way other non LinkedIn members will see it.

Tip #7: Add third-party applications to your profile.

One useful feature that many LinkedIn users fail to capitalize on is applying third-party applications to their profiles.

The default fields and boxes on LinkedIn can only tell so much. Even with great narratives and extensive texts about your skills and experience, you could lose out to other users who have taken the extra step to make their profiles more appealing to employers and contacts.

Although the third-party applications that LinkedIn offers aren't that many, these are still very useful applications that can showcase your portfolio, power point presentations and even a collaboration tool that lets you work on projects with your contacts.

Adding an application to your profile is easy.

On your Edit Profile page, scroll to the bottom of the page where you'll see the Applications section.

Click on the '+ Add an application' to see what applications are available for you to add on your profile.

The LinkedIn Applications Directory has 15 applications for you to choose from. Let's briefly discuss what these are:

> **Projects and Teamspaces by Manymoon**. A free "app" that lets you share tasks, projects and documents with your contacts. You will also be able to track the progress of your projects.

> **Polls by LinkedIn**. A useful app to help you gather "actionable data" from your contacts and networks.

SlideShare Presentations by SlideShare, Inc. Lets you upload power point presentations to your profile.

Lawyer Ratings by LexisNexis Martindale-Hubbell. A great addition for those in the legal industry. This app lets colleagues and clients leave reviews for lawyers.

My Travel by TripIt, Inc. A useful app if you want the opportunity to meet with your contacts and network face-to-face. You will be able to see your contacts' travel details and you can share yours as well.

E-Bookshelf by FT Press. This app will give you great reading materials regularly. The content is mostly for business and career improvements.

Reading List by Amazon by Amazon. Share your reading list with this app and get book recommendations from your contacts.

Portfolio Display by Behance. For graphic artists and design professionals, this app lets you upload unlimited multimedia to display on your profile.

Events by LinkedIn. You can schedule your own event or search for upcoming events posted by your contacts. If you want to take your professional relationship from LinkedIn to the real world, this app is perfect for the cause.

Real Estate Pro by Rofo. Staying up-to-date with the most recent real estate dealings and listings in your area as posted by active brokers and agents is easy with this app.

WordPress by WordPress. Link your blog with your LinkedIn profile to show your latest blog updates and posts.

Blog Link by SixApart. Not using WordPress for your blog? This app will let you connect your blog with your LinkedIn profile to show new posts and updates.

Legal Updates by JD Supra. Get easy access to the latest legal news in your area or country. You will also be able to upload your own articles and content which will be streamed to other Legal Updates app users.

Box.net Files by Box.net. This app lets you easily upload and manage your files online. You can also share those files with your contacts and network.

GitHub by LinkedIn. For programmers and coders, this app that lets you showoff your coding skills to other GitHub users. You can also collaborate with other users to come up with cool projects.

You can post multiple applications on your profile. However, you want to make sure that your profile is not too "cluttered" which can turn off interested employers. To add an application, follow these simple steps:

From the Applications Directory, choose the app that you wish to add and then click on its logo or link.

You will then be taken to the application's homepage. Here you will be able to read more about the app. You'll also see a preview of what the app looks like. When you have decided to add the application to your profile, click on the 'Add Application' button on the right side of the page.

Notice that there are two tick boxes above the 'Add Application' button. These are your options of how you want the app to be accessed, by you and your contacts.

If you don't want the app to be shown on your profile, just uncheck the corresponding box. You can change these settings later on.

After clicking on the 'Add Application' button, you will be taken to the application's startup page. Here, you will be able to make your first posts or to fix your settings. For the My Travel app, this is what you'll see:

Just follow the prompts that you'll see on the app that you added. You may need to sign up or create an account with the app's main site.

To see how the app looks on your profile, go to the Profile tab and then click on the 'View Profile' link.

Applications are typically located at the bottom of the page. You have the option to shuffle the boxes around your profile so that the applications can be easily seen. To do this, go to your Edit Profile page and then click on the section headings to move it around.

Choose the apps that you want to add carefully. Make sure that it ENHANCES you profile and complements the things about you that you want to promote.

Advanced Tips to Maximize Your LinkedIn Profile

Apart from the basic fields and third-party applications on LinkedIn, you can still do more to your profile to maximize and utilize the features that the site has to offer. Let's look at the different ways that you can improve your profile beyond the common customizations.

Add a Video to Your Profile

A lot of professionals overlook the usefulness of online videos in promoting their skills and services. According to a study published by Forbes, 65% of executives visit a vendor or supplier's page after seeing their online videos.

Videos make profiles more memorable. It is also a great method for you to show your skills like video editing or public speaking. If you feel like you can show more of what you can do through a short video, follow these simple steps to upload a video to your LinkedIn profile:

Upload your video to YouTube.

From your homepage, mouse over the 'More' tab and then click on the 'Get More
Applications' link.

Choose the SlideShare Presentations app from the Applications Directory.

Follow the steps we discussed in the previous section on how to add an application to your page. You will need to open a SlideShare account if you don't already have one.

Once you have added or linked SlideShare to your LinkedIn account, you will be taken to the app's homepage. Click on the 'Upload' button tab to begin uploading your video.

You'll be taken to the SlideShare's upload page. Click on the 'Browse and select files' button to begin.

Once your video file has been successfully uploaded, the next page that you'll see will allow you to set the title of your video and you may also include a short description.

If you don't want your contacts or network to download your video, uncheck the permission box as shown above.

After putting in your video title, tags and description, click on 'Publish' to begin conversion.

SlideShare will automatically convert your video to a LinkedIn-friendly format. Depending on the size and length of your video upload, this can take a few minutes or longer.

After the conversion is complete, click on the video to go to its main SlideShare video page. Once there, click on the 'Show on Profile' link for LinkedIn.

A popup confirmation box will appear to notify you that the last two uploaded presentations that are shown on your LinkedIn profile will be replaced by your video.

Check out your video on your LinkedIn profile page. Remember that you can rearrange the order of the sections in your profile if you want your SlideShare video to be more visible.

Visualize Your Resume

This time, we will use a third-party website with a LinkedIn application to make your resume more memorable and creative.

You may have noticed that infographics have become the Internet's latest information presentation tool. Through Vizualize.me, you can make your resume an infographic which can be accessed by your network through their newsfeed.

To get started, go to Vizualize.me's homepage. To save time, you can link your LinkedIn account with the site and they will simply grab the information that you posted on your profile. To do this, click on the 'Connect with LinkedIn' button.
Before you can proceed, you will need to give Vizualize.me permission to access your LinkedIn account.

The next page you'll see your Vizualize.me account homepage where the construction of your visual resume will take place. The site will ask you to provide an email address and a password to set up your own Vizualize account.

After setting up your account, you can create or modify your visual resume.

When you're done, the next step is to share your creation to your LinkedIn network. To do this, click on the 'Share' tab on the menu bar and then click on the LinkedIn icon.

Your infographic will be shared to your network as an update.

Use your own text to customize the post. When you're done, click on the 'Share' button.

You may also want to use LinkedIn to promote your business or to look for qualified employees to join your team. In the next chapter, you will learn how to establish a business page on LinkedIn and the different ways that the site can be used for varying purposes.

4. How to Use LinkedIn for your Business

LinkedIn is not only beneficial for job seekers and active professionals, it's also a great way to promote your business or company, an efficient recruitment tool and a reliable source of suppliers, contractors and investors.

Let's look at the steps you need to take in order to add your company to LinkedIn's growing directory of businesses.

Building a LinkedIn Profile for your Company

If you were able to create your personal LinkedIn profile effortlessly, then you'll have no problems in creating one for your business.

The first step is to add your company. On this page, you will be asked to fill out basic information about your company.

Fill in the information asked for and then click on the tick box. Hit 'Continue' button to proceed. You will be asked to confirm the e-mail address that you used to register your company.

After following the prompts on the verification e-mail sent to your inbox, click on the 'Confirm' button to arrive on the next page.

This is the page where you can set or edit the important details about your company. You will need to fill out all the required fields before you can publish your page.

For best results, ensure that all the fields are filled out with relevant, accurate and thorough information about your company. You will also need to designate an "admin" for the page. You may choose to be the page's administrator or you can delegate the task to other employees. You can have more than one admin for your page.

After publishing your profile, you will be taken to the Company Overview page.

From this page, you will be able to do several things:

- Post a job

- Add a product or service that will be highlighted on your company's page

- Review your followers' statistics

- Review your profile's statistics

- Take a closer look at your network and your employees' connections

As mentioned multiple times earlier, LinkedIn is used by hundreds of companies for recruitment. You too can tap this massive workforce for your own business. In the next section, we will look at how you can easily post jobs to fill in vacant positions in your company.

How to Use LinkedIn for Recruitment

There are millions of LinkedIn users, a lot of whom are highly qualified for any position that you need to fill in your company. To find the right person for the job, follow these simple steps:

From your company page, click on the 'Careers' tab.

On the first box, you will see the different advantages of posting a job on LinkedIn. Read through the short text and then click on the 'Post a Job' button under the photo.

You will be taken to the LinkedIn Jobs homepage. Click on the blue 'Post a Job' button on the slideshow at the top of the page.

You will then be taken to the page where you will lay out the details of your job posting. Remember that posting jobs on LinkedIn is NOT free. There are several price packages for you to choose from, depending on your location. The most common and widely used package is for a 30-day posting for $195. Rates are typically on a per job basis.

After filling out the details of your job listing, simply click on the 'Continue' button. LinkedIn will then give you a preview of the top applicants who match your requirements. For an additional $95, LinkedIn will fully disclose the top 24 qualified site members.

If you're committed to posting the job listing on LinkedIn, click on the 'Continue' button to proceed to the billing page. You can use your credit card to complete the payment.

When you're done paying for the posting, LinkedIn will send you a confirmation for your payment and your job listing.

Aside from recruitment, LinkedIn is a great platform to promote your business to your contemporaries, other businesses in your area or to potential investors. In the next section, you will be given tips on how to generate traffic for your LinkedIn company page and how you can use it as a marketing tool.

Tips on How to Promote your LinkedIn Page

In order to maximize the positive effects of your company's LinkedIn page, you'll need to actively promote and generate traffic to its profile. Let's explore the different techniques that you can use to advertise your page.

Edit your company page's URL to make it memorable and marketable.
LinkedIn allows its users – both individuals and entities to edit the URL of their pages to make it more personalized. Take advantage of this feature by using your company's name as the main URL extension of your business' LinkedIn page.

Include the company page's URL in your marketing collateral. Treat your company's LinkedIn page as you would your corporate website. Add the URL on your letterheads, brochures, corporate e-mail signatures, invoices, and other materials that gets distributed to your customers, clients and partners. If they have LinkedIn accounts, they will be able to follow your company page and subscribe to the updates that you'll post.

Add a "Follow Us" button on your website and other online content. It's easy to include a link to your company's LinkedIn page. In fact, LinkedIn provides a ready-made code that you can just copy and paste to your website.

You can also include the widget on the footer of your blog posts or articles that can be found on your website.

Use other social media platforms to promote your LinkedIn company page. If you already have a Twitter account and Facebook fan page for your company, use those platforms to advertise your LinkedIn page.

Having a good number of followers for your company's LinkedIn page will make it easier for you to promote your business and your product and service offerings. In the next section, we'll explore the different ways that you can use your company's LinkedIn page to increase inquiries and sales for your business.

How to Use Your Company's LinkedIn Page to Promote Your Business

You can use your company's LinkedIn page for a wide variety of purposes. We have already touched on using LinkedIn as a recruitment tool, it's now time for us to explore how you can use LinkedIn to promote your business and the products and services that you offer.

Follow these tips and tricks to generate more buzz for your business using your company's LinkedIn page.

Create and join groups. Being an active member of a LinkedIn group is an effective way to establish yourself or your company as an expert in your field. It is also a great way to meet other members who may want to visit your company's page.

Finding and searching for groups is easy, just mouse over the 'Groups' tab on the LinkedIn menu bar to see your options.

From there, you can look for groups that you deem relevant to your interests or you can start your own group and invite people from your network.

Integrate your Twitter feed. A lot of companies take advantage of Twitter's simple features that allows them to make short posts about their products and services. You can harness the potential of Twitter by integrating it with your LinkedIn page. The updates that you make from Twitter will be distributed to your network via the Network Updates feed on the homepage.

Make your network updates count. When posting status updates for your company's LinkedIn page, be sure that it's something that will grab the attention and pique the interest of your network and contacts. You can promote your products, highlight features or simply post news and company-related updates. You will need to prepare catchy and attention-grabbing product copies to make your promotion more effective.

Get your employees involved. Encourage your employees to create LinkedIn profiles and to list your company as their employer. Give them product copies and sales materials that they can use for their own status updates. These updates will be visible on their networks as well. With just one status update per employee, you can potentially reach over 10,000 people. Just be careful not to overdo it. Aggressive selling and advertising on LinkedIn can get you flagged as a spammer.

Maximize the Products and Services page. Each company profile on LinkedIn has its own Products and Services page where businesses can highlight what they offer.

Using this feature, you can also receive recommendations from your clients and customers who are LinkedIn members. This is an effective way to establish the credibility of your business. It's no secret that most people would patronize a brand if their friends and contacts recommend it. This is LinkedIn's version of word-of-mouth marketing and it is just as effective.

Be sure to use professional photos of your products, as much as possible. High quality material will give your business more legitimacy. Also include concise yet memorable product descriptions for each item that you upload to your page.

Reply to comments from your network. This is a very simple and easy step that is often overlooked by business and company owners. Your contacts and network will be able to leave comments on the status updates that you publish. This is a great way to encourage a dialog between the company and the people who follow it. This is also a useful method of generating leads for your business. Users who frequently comment on your material will be easier to approach through private messaging should the need arises.

Engage your audience. If you want your contacts to be interested in what you have to offer, you have to publish material that would grab their attention. If you have other marketing materials that you use for your website or social media campaigns, you can also use them for your LinkedIn page. Add applications to your page or at the very least, provide links to where they can access photos or videos about your products.

You can also encourage discussions and exchanges of ideas between your contacts. Ask probing and leading questions through your status updates. The more time people spend checking for your updates, the easier it will be for you to promote your business.

Don't expect to be an instant hit on LinkedIn because these types of social media campaigns take time. It's important for you to manage your expectations and to set goals for what you want to achieve on LinkedIn. Many businesses have flourished using this professional networking site. You know have the tools and the knowledge at your disposal to attract the same success for your own company and your career.

5. Conclusion

LinkedIn has become an essential social networking platform for professionals and business-oriented individuals. Having a LinkedIn profile has become a necessity if you want to have a robust network at your disposal for any professional purpose that you may need.

Individuals have flocked to LinkedIn because of the number of employment and career opportunities that it offers. If you want to stay ahead of the competition, you'll need to ensure that your LinkedIn profile has all the information that a recruiter needs to know about your skills and experience.

Companies and businesses have also realized the great potential that LinkedIn can offer for their bottom line. Recruiters and headhunters use LinkedIn because of the sheer magnitude of the pool of qualified professionals just waiting to be found. It is also a cheaper and more efficient alternative in searching for skilled workers. If you have a company with some positions to fill, LinkedIn can provide you with cost-effective recruitment solutions.

LinkedIn is also a good platform that you can use to promote your company and the products and services that you offer. There are plenty of available features that you can take advantage of, even with the free and basic account. All it takes is creativity and patience for you to unlock the full potential of LinkedIn.
If you want to maximize your reach using LinkedIn, the best way to do it is to add contacts to your page. Even with less than 20 contacts, you can still connect with over 800,000 professionals all over the world. With a little bit of effort and some ingenuity, you can get your profile noticed by the right people. Building a successful career is possible with LinkedIn.

6. THANK YOU FOR READING!

Thank You so much for reading this book. If this title gave you a ton of value, It would be amazing for you to leave a REVIEW !

THANK YOU FOR DOWNLOADING! IF YOU ENJOYED THIS BOOK AND WOULD LIKE TO READ MORE TITLES FROM MY COLLECTION CLICK THIS LINK

www.ingramcontent.com/pod-product-compliance
Lightning Source LLC
Chambersburg PA
CBHW051216050326
40689CB00008B/1339